Life's Path

Suzanne Henderson

BookLeaf Publishing

India | USA | UK

Presentation by *BookLeaf Publishing*

Web: www.bookleafpub.com

E-mail: info@bookleafpub.com

ISBN: 9789358315769

First edition 2023

DEDICATION

I write this book to you, the reader. I hope you will find a little something in these pages to help you along in your own personal journey of life.

ACKNOWLEDGEMENT

Thank you to all the people who encouraged me in my writing and spurred me on. You know who you are and I love you and appreciate you.

PREFACE

I was inspired to write these poems as I went through a time of change in my life. As I realised that Life's Path often takes us on unexpected twists and turns, I started to look closer at what was around me and, through pain and through joy, I found words for my experience. I hope you will join me in discovering the why for your journey.

Once I Was

Once I was small and slight
young and small
vulnerable and scared
at the mercy of their might.

Once I was confused and lost
driven by fear
lost in the snow
the drifts so deep.

I didn't know I'd sunk below
their own expectations
of what life should be
I was only doing my best.

Once I was so silent and mute
a puppet of artistry made for show.
I walked the walk and said the words
with syllables I didn't believe
while inside a big shout was held
waiting to escape and drown
out their world with sound so loud.
Maybe I wasn't just small and cute
and they would know soon.

Once I was so sad and low

yet a smile and laughter would I bestow
as I drew pictures of sun and light
and then sat alone as the darkness came
and wondered if I might disappear soon
and perhaps, perhaps it would be so!

Once I was, but now I am.
I am the me I always was
trapped beneath the layers of soil
waiting to emerge one day.
And the sun it helped me grow, it did
and soon my eyes would open up
to the beauty of the world
and I could say that is what I was.

Once I was, but now here I am
and it is with joy I scream my name.
I stand so tall, I speak with strength
and pushing through the broken strands of life
I speak and cry and shout with truth.
No longer words of others do I speak
they are my own, said without shame.

Now I am. Reborn, like a flower springing forth
and no longer do I wilt with fear
from their might and raised spear of words.
Instead with grace I lift my head
and own my space in this soil
the ground that I was born to own.

My world, my space, this air to breathe
I do, I do now know my worth!

New Dawn

I woke up to the sound of bird song, that sweet happy trill. It made my heart sing, it made me long for new.

It made me long for new.

New skies, new paths, new hope. The bird told me of a new day, spreading all across the globe. He told me with his song; hear it with me.

My limbs were heavy, my heart was weak, tears stung my eyes, and hope was nowhere within my view.

But I woke up to birdsong. That sweet bright sound. A new day had arrived. I was alive, alive and no longer alone. Take my hand; walk with me.

New skies, new paths, new hope. The birdsong told me of a new day spreading all across the globe.

Sometimes life is dark. Sometimes life is hard.
Sometimes no one can be found in that lonely
place I go to hide.

But a new day is here. The birdsong opened my
heart.

Listen to the music. Beautiful music. No matter
what a new day can be found.

And it's in the birdsong. It's in the breeze. It's in
the green beneath our feet. Listen to the sound.

New skies, new paths, new day. The birdsong
told of a new day spreading all across the globe.

Hope is here to stay.
Sing along with me.
Let's join the birdsong...
Let's take to the skies.
Let's fly.

Beginnings

So, what now you ask as the sun sets? You pick up your dreams and put them in a box, a box labelled later, and stare up at the galaxies and wonder at it all, what is the meaning of this?

So, what now you ask as you watch that door close, and turn away, picking up your heart as it falls to the floor, feeling the grip of despair, the ending of another start. It seemed so right, it seemed to call, and now it all seems so morose.

So, what now you ask as the darkness sets in and no one else is around. You're alone, and feel so far from all you knew. The phone is dead, the emails have stopped, the house is silent, a living grave of regret. You wonder how a room can echo with no sound.

So, what now you ask as he walks away, his steps an echo, his voice fading. Like the memories you built, all just a dream captured on a lens. You flick through the photos, you read the old texts and none of it seems like it happened to you. Because he's gone and you feel so bereft.

So, what now you ask as the empty nest
syndrome sets in. The silence of a house once
filled with so much joy and sound. The children
gone, will they remember the days you built
around them? Will they sleep and dream of you
too? It feels, it feels, it feels like an end.

So, what now you ask as your new life starts
with the new day ahead of you. The sun still
shines and sets in time, the flowers sprout and
remember to flower. The birds wake you up with
the morning dawn and tell you it's a new day, get
up! And you do because you can, and you pause
at the edge of life and wonder what to sow.

So, what now you ask and life answers your cry,
if you ask with an open mind. Life goes on,
times will change, and people and seasons never
stand still. So, pick up your dreams, pick up
your heart and remember again who you are.
Take one step, and then another. See the path
open up? It's yours to take.

So, don't be scared, don't be sad, not for too
long, don't waste this life. Take each day, the
new and the old, take the other path if this one is
closed. Open your heart, sing with the dawn, lift
up your courage and know you're okay. And take

a step, just one at a time. So, what now? That is
for you to choose.

Falling in Love Again

I was lost, I was broken
I didn't know how to live
Until I listened to my heart
And this is what it said.

Fall in love again
Dream of peace
Walk hand in hand with joy
Pick berries from the tree of gratitude
... Open your hands to receive

Fall in love again
With what you once knew
To be your heart content
... Remember it

Fall in love again
With the joy of music
The glory of a crisp new book
The buzz of a creative thought exploding into
life
Feel it
Again
.. Feel it

Fall in love again.
Walk out into the crisp night air
Look up at the stars
Feel the earth under your feet
Grab at the world's oxygen
Enfold it into your lungs
... And breathe

Fall in love again
With the freedom of your bones
Let your body dance to music
Let it go
... Express your soul

Fall in love again
With your open book
The new day calling
The new friends to meet
... Run to it with open arms

Fall in love again
With this. With life.
Life as you know it
Imperfect and messy and painful and beautiful
... Grasp it

Fall in love again with this one day
The sunrise of its awakening
The sunshine and the storms of its moods

The darkness, the stars of its slumber
The sunset of its goodnight
... Love it all

Fall in love again with life
Your one life. Yours to use. Yours to spend
Stand in your light and accept this gift
The gift of the present.
... Take it.

Monday Blues

When all the darkness is in the sky, when my
feet feel heavy and my heart is low and
everything says Monday and nothing says joy.

I look up and see the bird as it swoops. I see the
colour of the river flow by. I imagine the fish
swimming below, their world a myriad of
beautiful hues.

And I look at the stranger who smiles as I pass,
and I breathe the air, oxygen to my lungs. I listen
for the song of the bird as it draws near and look
at the leaves as they turn orange-gold.

And suddenly I'm glad to have a Monday; with
all its bad vibes it's still a day. A day of
possibility, a day with a view, a day with a song
in it for me.

And my head might be full of so much to do,
and I might not have slept too well at all, and I
might have hated the Monday at first as I
grimaced at its clock face and hated its chores.

But I soon loved Monday because it lit up with a day more to live and a blessing to find, and I promise this Monday as it draws to a close, that next week I will welcome it with a smile and some joy!

She Danced Again

She used to dance like a young deer, she used to dance so free. She used to spin across the floor, the joy evident to see.

But there came a day when she stopped, she came to a dark time, and she stumbled and dropped to the floor as the world around her slowed.

The days went on, as life will do, whatever you do with it, but behind her door, the fear grew and her feet lay still and heavy.

She walked, she tried to put her feet, one behind the other, but each day as the sun came up, her heart was so, so heavy.

She heard music, she heard the sound, and saw others dance so free, but somehow the magic went and she couldn't hear or see like she had before.

But one day some magic happened as she picked up all her courage and she walked out onto the open floor and let herself spin faster.

Faster and freer, she became the sound, the
music was her master and she was floating high
as air as she began to dance again.

Courage and hope were all it took to dance
again, she found, and as she spun she had great
joy and the world was so much brighter.

Learning to Fall

I tried to stand and not fall because the ground
seemed so hard, a dangerous place to be, the
place below my feet. I felt so small, because I
was so afraid to fall.

I tried to stabilise, to keep my balance, even
while the world swayed before my eyes. I
wanted to look tall; I wanted to be strong, but I
clung so tight to walls, so afraid to fall.

I was told I was doing well, that I was climbing
high, but it only made me fear; I knew what lay
beneath, because I had started there, and I was
not fearless.
I knew that I could fall, and all I had be gone; so
dizzying was my fear, so afraid to fall.

Each day was no fun, trapped on a
merry-go-round, I dreamed, I climbed, I worked
so hard, while clinging tight with aching limbs,
and nothing was any fun; I guess I knew why, I
was just so afraid to fall.

But gravity has a law, and it never fails to win,
and so one day to the ground I fell with one
almighty crash.

I hurt from head to toe; it really stung so much
and I knew I had to get back to my feet if I
wanted to overcome. Yet it took such courage, it
really did. Because I knew how much it hurt; I
was so afraid to fall.

But to my feet I got; that was the bravest thing
I'd ever done and although no applause was
heard, I knew I'd really won. I'd made myself
proud, getting up from the ground, and my step
was so much surer after that.

I had learned one big lesson; to learn to walk, to
run, to climb; to win that fight
that we call life, there is one lesson we must
conquer first; we must learn how to fall.

Slow Down

When the pace is too hard and you're feeling worn down. When your heart is screaming but you're too tired to sleep. When the world is too bright and too loud and too fast, it's okay to slow down today.

When you've used all your strength and you've given your all, and there is nothing but emptiness screaming at you. When you want to give more but you are weary of trying, it's okay to slow down today.

When you don't feel enough, because more is always the cry, when putting one foot in front of the other is a challenge for you, it's okay to slow down today.

When you feel challenged, when you feel taxed, when everyone seems to be asking of you, asking much more than you're able to give, I wonder who's doing the asking. Could it be you? It's okay to slow down today.

Speak to your heart, listen inside, take those deep breaths and feel you're alive. Do what gives

joy, take it easy today, because you're important,
just here as you are. It's okay to slow down
today.

And the world will move on and do its thing
whatever the pace you adopt. But when the
voice that's inside is screaming help me I'm lost,
you must, yes you must, slow down.

Your Shoes

Could I walk in your shoes just for a day
Could I borrow the confidence you seem to
assume
Could I use your eyes to look the world in the
eye
Could I borrow your world.
Just once
Just once.

Could I borrow your memories of happy days
Could I borrow the glow of confidence grown
Could I steal your world
Just for one day
Could I walk please could I walk
In your shoes just for one day.

You wear your shoes with confidence
You walk in a way that owns the ground
You smile and laugh and hold your head high
No one can bring you down from that height.
I look up from the ground below your feet
I find it hard to meet your eye
I hear you say be confident girl
I hear you say believe in yourself.

I try to do as you say, as I walk in my shoes
But I slip and I stumble and I forget my steps
So I turn to you and I say please can I borrow
Please can I steal please can I know
What it is to walk in your shoes
Just for one day.

But you say no, you say it can't be done
My shoes, my way, my path, my day
Are all I can have, I have to pave my way
Live your life you say, take that step.

And so I put on my shoes for another day
I walk in steps so familiar to me
And I look in the mirror and say to myself
Can I walk in your shoes just for one day
With hope and pride and joy to be me.

Could you walk in my shoes just for one day
Because I have much to show you by the way
My shoes may be small, my steps so slow
My fear holding me back from all I dream
But I have much to show, much to teach
If you'd only walk in my shoes for just one day.

The War

Revenge is not the way, karma is not needed is
what I say.

You look a bit shocked, calm down and listen,
for this is why I feel forgiveness is key.

That person hurt you, that guy is not fair, that
woman dug a knife in your back.
You turn with a savage look in your eye, but let
me explain why revenge won't do.

That person is hurting, that guy has been
wronged, that woman is fighting a war of her
own. Take a step back and look in their eye; do
they really look happy to you?

I know that they shouldn't have hurt you like
that; they are vicious and cruel, it is true, they
have a cold heart and sharp nails and they dug
them into you.

But take a step back and ask yourself this; do
you really want their disease? It is hidden in
anger, resentment and fear, and if you respond

back in anger I'm afraid that you are ill with it
too.

So I'm asking if there is a better way to mend
this, better than wishing for their demise?
Because as you turn and throw coals on their
head, the fire sparks back and it hurts you too.

So what do I do, you ask in surprise. Well, let's
walk away from that devil in disguise. It's
hidden in resentment and fear and anger and it's
going to kill you before it kills them.

Let's sit down in peace and say you forgive. Just
try to mean it, I know it sounds big. The more
that you say it, the more you will mend and soon
the forgiveness you speak will turn and heal you.

That person will find her own path, that guy will
suffer for his own sins, that woman will stab
herself in the back. Trust me, just leave them to
their own way.

But wish them the best, wish them the world,
and as you pray for their safety and walk away,
the peace that you earn will be with you.

You don't have to take their angry words, but
you don't have to respond in the same way.

You have a weapon in your own hands. It's
strong and it's mighty and it works all the time.
It's called love and forgiveness and it's also
called peace, and it starts first with you.

So give yourself love, give yourself respect and
walk away from those people who don't give the
same.

And soon you will see, if you follow this path,
that revenge is not needed and you are set free.

Music to my Ears

Words materialised from your pen, notes strung
from instrument chords. Volume bouncing from
a speaker tall, ears opened to a magical sound.

Sitting people rise to the tune, feet tapping like
something possessed, heads lift, hands tap, no
one can deny its power; ears opened to a magical
sound.

Dance floor full, seats empty, feet glide, hands
touch, people drawn into each other, connecting,
notes detected, ears opened to a magical sound.

Far away from the tune that is strumming,
people smile and nod to one another; memories
stir, eyes moisten, ears opened to a magical
sound.

Sitting alone, mood grey, hands in fists and brow
furrowed, I hear the notes and want you near as
my ears are opened to a magical sound.

Notes strumming, an arrow from a bow hits the
heart and I'm undone. I rise and pick up the

phone, knowing I don't want to be alone, ears opened to a magical sound.

You are dazzling, eyes are bright, as I take your hand tonight. And the lights shimmer and dance to the tune, as our ears are opened to a magical sound.

All the past is forgotten, all that matters is now, as you pull close to me and we melt to a tune. The music is magic, it's mending our hearts, ears opened to a magical sound.

It is at the end as the music dies and all is silent and darkness falls around, that you draw close and whisper a song with three words and my heart fills up with joy as my ears are opened to a magical sound.

Shadows

Shadows dance across my path, I can't discern what is real and what is fake. Memories and dreams, nightmares and trials, causing an overgrowth in my mind. Which road do I take?

Shadows dance across your face. I cannot tell what is real and what is fake. I want to ask but know not how, and instead I hide and let the questions race.

The sunlight breaks and I can see. The shadows move and dive away. I do not have to be afraid of questions and of dying dreams, I simply have to look for the light. And in the morning I am free, to dream new dreams and live my hopes.

I choose it now, I choose the light. I choose to hope and live my dreams. They often shift, they often dart, like fireflies into the night. But always, always, if I keep the faith, and do not let the shadows pull my gaze, I see hope return like the breaking dawn and I will find the road if I walk with strength.

Doubts are shadows that can steal your joy if you let them have their way. Don't let them win, keep your lamp of hope and do not ever hide that light. You are the light, you are your hope, and you need never feel alone. And soon you will see, as the shadows leave, that you are the guide who brought you safe home.

Broken Mirrors

I know a lot of women, I am one of them, who would hate the mirror, an enemy of me.

We dress it up, we dress it down, hating how hard it is to be a stunner. And we measure everything on that blessed critic on the wall there.

We bounce out of bed and try to hide our wobble. Goodness where did that extra button go, and the guy in the bed better hadn't catch us naked. The mirror is enough of a judge and it's telling us we're double!

We slide to the kitchen to make a cup of coffee, while berating ourselves for ingesting one more calorie. That message on the fridge reminds us of the mirror, the one which said we were too fat and had to do much better.

We dress in front of the mirror and gasp in horror, whispering I really wish I was a little slimmer. We adjust the lighting and breathe in until the world goes a little darker, and pull on

clothes that hide the real us from the people who
would admire us.

As we switch on the TV the women greet us
who are everything we're not. I wonder if their
mirror tells them they are perfect or if they are
just the same as us, dear. And on social media
we grimace and use a filter to hide our smile
lines, dreaming of the day when we can be so
much fitter.

We hurry down the street, pulling at our hair
and, catching a glimpse of a stray, we try to hide
behind a curtain. We catch admiring glances and
take them for judgment because that mirror on
the wall said I was looking tired.

But I wonder if today we threw that broken
mirror out, and asked each other for the truth of
what we see. I wonder what we'd find, I wonder
how much we'd smile. Because I know that the
beauty that shines through you, no mirror can
ever do it justice.

Choose Life

Such a fool dancing with death
the beauty of his eyes
the dance of my life.

His lies sound like the truth
his fingers of ice stroke my cheek
he shows me a dream
he sells me a hope
written in a contract of blood.

And I don't see the lies
I don't see the danger
although it's written all over the walls.
I swallow the wine red as blood
and the world begins to shimmer and shine.

I see my mistake as the darkness falls
and the triumph in his eyes as I struggle for air.
I sleep the dream of the tortured dead
and wake to a world that is broken and torn.

He calls again and I like a puppet go
to the world of the frozen and drugged
and he takes my health, he takes my hope,
bit by bit, straw by straw.

But he tells me a lie only the insane believe
I am that one, I have bought his tale.

It takes strength to scream for help
to the people around who run to my aid.
They pick me up, and they pull me away, from
the broken fake diamonds and the grip of his
hand.

I wake with a gulp, with a breath of pure air.
and I reach out to the light, I lift my head up.
And when I turn towards that beam
the darkness withers, it cannot stay.

I have a choice. It is my decision.
The light or the dark, the narrow path to life or
the wide path to death.
I chose the light. I chose the narrow path,
The one less travelled, the one that hurts.

And as I walk the lighter it gets
and soon I am skipping and singing with joy.
I choose life. I choose life. And those lies of
death, I will not hear.

Come with me. Take my hand.
Please choose life. Choose life with me.

Waiting Game

I used to hate the waiting game
the time I spent just hanging on
for the doorbell to ping
for the oven to do its thing.

Waiting is a part of life
it's part of the strife.
It can also be part of the joy.
Joy in the waiting.

We wait in queues, we wait in lines
we listen for the postman.
We wonder how long it will be before
this or that will happen.

We hang our hopes on that waiting game
and sit impatiently for life's calling.
We push the accelerator to the floor
and sigh in exasperation.
But life waits for no man and the clock is
demanding.
Impatience for the next moment is a wasting of
the current.
So as I sit and wait, my foot about to tap
to skip the hour on

I take a breath and look around
soaking in this second
and remember how to smile and sing
and dream in colour in this moment.

Let's enjoy the wait
let's enjoy the journey
let's enjoy the walk from here to there
and let's soak it in
this world we're in.
It's there in every moment.

The Writer's Curse

The writing urge can be a bit like a curse. In sleeping hours my muse appears, tugging at my sleeve saying it is time to play.

In a meeting serious she dances around, and leads me astray with her playful words. I open the window and follow the words over fields and streets and down into the dark. I never know where she will lead, but I'm intoxicated and follow that way.

I never quite know when she will appear, taking me on a journey for hours. A character of imagination may appear, a vision, a scene, a word or more. And then I'm off and following that path.

But searching for her sometimes can be a bore for she doesn't always come when I call. I can sit in the quiet and search for the words while she hides behind a stone or a wall.

That is when I throw down the pen and cry, a writer? I will never be that, and I sigh. Then she will reappear and off we will go, on a magical

journey it could be anywhere at all! It's a
miracle, it's a joy and I love to write, I do!

So that writing muse, that annoying writing
muse; I doubt her existence until she appears
and tells me we are starting again, and I have no
choice, I have no voice.

She is my master. My writing muse.

So forgive my madness, forgive my distraction,
forgive my forays into imagination and such.

I have no choice, I have to follow, that writing
muse, wherever she goes.

Camera Angles

I'm the one behind the camera. They can't see
me but I'm here. I'm in charge of the angle, the
lighting and can make things disappear.

Say cheese and smile and tilt your head that
way. Let me get a little closer. Ahh don't be shy.

I'm the one behind the camera. I'm the one who
watches on, who picks out your good side and
takes the best shot.

I'm the one behind the camera. It's me you're
smiling at. Your husband is beside you but it's
me who's watching on. And you know you need
me here, to tell the world you're happy, even if
you're not.

I'm the one behind the camera. I'm quite happy
here. I'm hidden in the shadows, the dark is
where I produce my best art.

I'm the one behind the camera. I tell stories with
these clips, I can smudge out your tears or make
your day a ruin, with just a little slip.

I'm the one behind the camera. I see the colours
and the joy. See the kingfisher rise in splendour,
and watch the sun as it sets.

I'm the one behind the camera. But it's getting
lonely here. Can I move into your photo please,
let's pose and make the image glow.

I'm the one in the picture. Let's post the images
for the world to see. Let them ask the question,
who's taking the photo now?

He's the one with the camera. I think he's found
us out. I guess now we are going to have to find
a safer place to hide.

Yes, he's the one with the camera. He says you're
looking happier, as he cries. Well, they do
indeed say that the camera never lies.

The Magic of the Years

It dipped in the middle, its spine bowing from
the years, time had rendered it an old and
battered chair. I sat on the edge and slid right to
its middle, where it cuddled me in silence and
told me some tales.

It had only been in this room, it hadn't travelled
far. Its heavy legs and straight-backed stance
held it firm to its place. But it had seen many
things, over so many years, so many people had
lingered on its lap.

It had seen the warmth of sunlight, dappling
through that window, scorching and fading the
leather of its skin. It had heard the laughter of
children, little legs jumping and leaping across
its body and had held a newborn baby as its
mother sat close by.

It had held up an elderly man, his bones
creaking as he sat, and listened to his memories
as he sat and pondered there.

So many secrets had been shared over a cuppa sitting on that chair, and so many tears shed, both joy and pain it had seen.

It had seen so many cold winters, the open fire spitting so near to its skin, as the storm raged outside, knocking and keening at the window.

It felt so weary now. Its skin was old and wrinkled, the leather of old melting as it sat. It still held me as I lingered there, and told me it wouldn't let me fall, and that its legs were still as strong as the day they were carved.

It could have gone for scrap, when I bought the house, but instead I put a cover over it and restuffed its cushions. I took a duster and polished out its deepest flaws and then sat and admired it, grand, and proud it really was.

Its skin was so old I could never iron out those years. Memories etched so deep, why should they ever be lost?

I put new photos on the table and my own decorations all around, but I promised that the old sofa it would stay with all its charm. Because it reminded me of us, in our human skin, the older we get the more we have to share.

Don't hide those broken pieces, don't ever say
you're old and past your best. Just celebrate your
beauty and the magic.

The magic of the years.

Don't Look Back

And as you move into your new chapter, as you leave the past behind, as you run towards your future, don't look back at what you leave.

The past is paved with pain and with some joy too. Put a memento in your pocket, and throw a kiss to the history you shared. But don't linger there, look forward and be glad. Because you don't live in history, it's a brand new story now.

The way to run a marathon, the way to climb a hill, is to always look before you.,or else you will fall down. So keep moving forward, the path behind is gone, and there's no need to cover old ground...the new is up ahead.

You can keep photos on your walls, you can celebrate the good that went before, and sometimes there will be tears when you remember who you left behind. But dear please don't sit there, lamenting the past, for time is ticking on and there is so much for you to do.

With a spring in your step and hope in your
heart, look forward to the future...look ahead and
not behind.

The View Over There

Other people's lives, seen through a camera lens. Blown up and distorted; your life minimised, destroyed. Catastrophic imaginings, and fantastic beliefs, are seen through the lens of a colourful view.

As you walk into the greyness of another sky, you wonder why the sun always shines over there. You run with your dreams to fall flat on your face, while overhead an aeroplane takes the lucky away.

Your heart is heavy as a stone; you dream of the day when your life will be as amazing as the girl on TV. You write a letter to the stars and ask that next year you can be anyone, anything, other than you. So fearless and free. So happy and light. Please let me be anything but me.

The clock on your wall counts the minutes down with a sigh, and you tap your fingers and try to catapult yourself into the skies. But your legs are heavy and your heart won't fly. You frown as the seconds take away your life breath, and you seethe that someone else is living your dream.

You spend your time away from your desk
scrolling your phone just to check that others
really are having the best time they can have.
You envy their lifestyle, that skin so sublime,
that perfect relationship written all over their
face. They have plans for the summer full of ice
cream and fun, and parties that you could never
afford. Everything is perfect for those on your
screen. But here you're having the worst
nightmare day.

Maybe one day you'll wake up and notice the
sun on your path. You'll see that the bird is
singing just for you. The normal and drear is
filled with such cheer. Because you've noticed
that no one's life is better than yours.

Don't waste one more minute of your precious
time wishing for better, wishing for more. Don't
scroll social media thinking they have it just so.
Because it's not the truth, dear, I have to say.
Instead, use every minute to make your dreams
come true. Paint your perfect picture and walk
onto your screen. And don't worry who's
watching, what tales they're telling of you.
Remember you were in their shoes once,
watching others have the time of their lives.

Life

She fell in love with the stillness. The loudness of a ticking clock, the silence of early morning, the darkness of the night, cosy and safe.

And she remembered all she had not done before. One by one she picked those experiences up like pebbles on a beach, tried them in her palm, and walked into those new happenings, breathing and feeling and seeing life.

And she remembered all she had done before. She discarded the bad and photographed the good, framing those memories on her wall, and crowning them with thanks.

She walked barefoot over a beach, she swam in the sea, she breathed in the cold, cold air in winter, she let the sun melt her skin in summer, and she felt it. She felt it all.

She watched herself grow older, the gentling of her features, the wrinkle of skin around her eyes, and was glad.

And she opened her heart, a little more each day,
to the good, to the bad, to the pain and to the joy.
She let herself feel, and she let herself be. She
loved.

Yes she saw the difference between living and
dying, happiness and sadness. And she saw
choices in her mornings and decisions in her
evenings. She turned the pages of her world with
reverence and delved into the book with
abandon.

And she let the clock tick and she let the world
turn, she lived as she did and she let others live.
She discovered the beauty below the soil and she
let life teach her what it would. She let herself
fly and she let herself fall. And she wrote it all
down and learned from it all.

At the end of her days, she smiled and said, I'm
so glad I chose to live and experience it all.
Once upon a time, I made that choice, I either
die completely or I live free. And live I have, it's
here etched on my face, in the palms of my
hands and the corneas of my eyes. And now I
can go with peace, knowing I chose life and life
chose me.